What Did the Fishermen Catch?
and other Questions

By Sally Ann Wright • Illustrated by Paola Bertolini Grudina

What did Abraham want?

A baby son!

God had promised him a huge family, as many children as stars in the sky. But it was many years before his wife Sarah had baby Isaac. Then God blessed them with grandchildren and great grandchildren – a very big family.

What did Esau eat?

A bowl of lentil soup!

Esau had been out all day and was so hungry, he told his younger brother he would give anything to eat what he was cooking.
So Jacob gave him the soup.
But in return Esau gave him the special blessing that a father gave only to his first son.

What did Joseph wear?

A beautiful colored coat!

It made his brothers so jealous that
they made sure he was sent away
to a strange land to live.
But God had plans for Joseph.
God kept Joseph safe in Egypt
so he could help his family many years later.

What did the princess find?

A baby in a basket!

Moses was hidden there to keep him safe from the soldiers.

The princess wanted to keep him.
So she let him grow up in the palace.
When Moses was grown up,
God helped him to save his people.

What did Solomon build?

A beautiful temple!

Solomon loved God so much
he wanted to build a beautiful building
so people could come to worship him.
Solomon chose the finest wood
and the best silver and gold
to make a very special gift for God.

What did the shepherds see?

Angels in the sky!

The shepherds were looking after their sheep
when the angels came to tell them
that baby Jesus had been born in Bethlehem.
They ran to see the special baby
who would bring peace to the world,
and found him lying in a manger.

What did the fishermen catch?

Lots of fish!

Peter and Andrew had caught nothing all night but Jesus told them to let down their nets in the deeper water of lake Galilee.

What did the soldier need?

A word from Jesus!

The Roman soldier had a servant who was very ill.
The soldier didn't want to bother Jesus.
He didn't even need him to come to his house!

"I know you can help," the soldier said.
"Just say the word and my servant will be well."
So Jesus did – and the soldier's servant got better.

What did the huge crowd share?

Bread and fish!

Thousands of people had been listening to Jesus. Jesus saw that they were hungry and wanted to help. A boy had a basket of five rolls and two little fish.

The boy gave his basket to Jesus.
Jesus thanked God and shared the food...
and everyone had enough to eat and some left over!

What did the kind man do?

Helped his neighbor!

Jesus told a story about a dying man.
First a priest walked past without helping.
Then another religious man did the same.
It was a man from another country who stopped,
washed the man's wounds, and put him on his own donkey.
Jesus said that this man pleased God.

What did the leper say?

Thank you!

Jesus met ten men
who had a skin disease.
They couldn't live normal lives.
No one would come near them.
So when they asked him,
Jesus made them well.
Nine men went away,
happy to be healed.
Only one came back to thank Jesus.

What did the widow give?

Everything she had!

The rich men gave lots of money to the Temple.
But they still had plenty left over.
Jesus told his disciples that the widow had given more than any of them.
Her two copper coins were all she had,
but she had given them to God.

What did Jesus ride?

A donkey!

Two of the disciples put cloaks over the donkey's back.
Jesus sat on it and rode into Jerusalem.
Crowds of people were going there for the festival.
They spread their cloaks on the ground.
They waved palm branches in the air.
"Hooray for Jesus the king!"
they shouted.

Copyright © 2006 by Anno Domino Publishing Services Ltd
1 Churchgates, The Wilderness, Berkhamsted, Herts HP4 2UB

Text copyright © 2006 by Paulist Press, Inc., Sally Ann Wright
Illustrations copyright © 2006 by Paola Bertolini Grudina

All rights reserved. No part of this book may be reproduced or transmitted in any form or by any means, electronic or mechanical, including photocopying, recording or by any information storage and retrieval system without permission in writing from the Publisher.

Stories can be found in the Bible as follows:
What did Abraham want? Genesis 12:1-2; 21:1-7
What did Esau eat? Genesis 25:27-33
What did Joseph wear? Genesis 37, 46
What did the princess find? Exodus 2:1-10
What did Solomon build? 1 Kings 6:1-38
What did the shepherds see? Luke 2:8-16
What did the fishermen catch? Luke 5:1-11
What did the soldier need? Matthew 8:5-13
What did the huge crowd share? John 6:1-13
What did the kind man do? Luke 10:30-37
What did the leper say? Luke 17:11-19
What did the widow give? Luke 21:1-4
What did Jesus ride? Mark 11:1-10

Cataloging-in-Publication Data from the Library of Congress is available on request.

ISBN: 0-8091-6732-8

Published in the United States by Paulist Press
997 Macarthur Boulevard, Mahwah, NJ 07430

www.paulistpress.com

Printed and bound in Singapore